For My Brother Peter

Thanks to everyone that has helped me to get here.

thanks for Pornocchio photo by Jason Garrity

Cover script by. Nicholas Frederick *

Shower curtain Models Mia & Emily Eve

And thanks to my Highschool for making things

so Boring I drew everyday instead of Algebra,

Couldn't of dun it width out yu guis sf

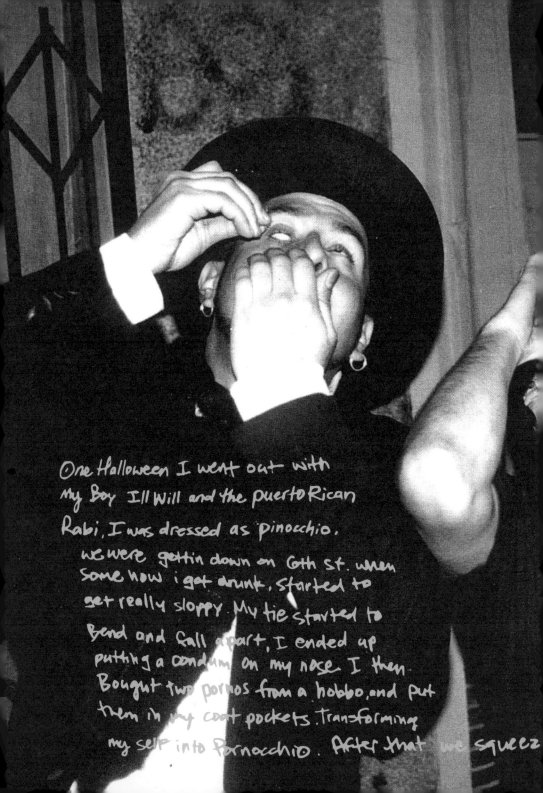

One Halloween I went out with
my Boy Ill Will and the puerto Rican
Rabi, I was dressed as 'pinocchio.
we were gettin down on 6th st. when
some how i get drunk, started to
get really sloppy. My tie started to
bend and fall apart, I ended up
putting a condum on my nose. I then.
Bought two pornos from a hobbo, and put
them in my coat pockets. Transforming
my self into Pornocchio. After that we squeez

mes in our
eyes.

The Jacking Tree

by

Sam florestein

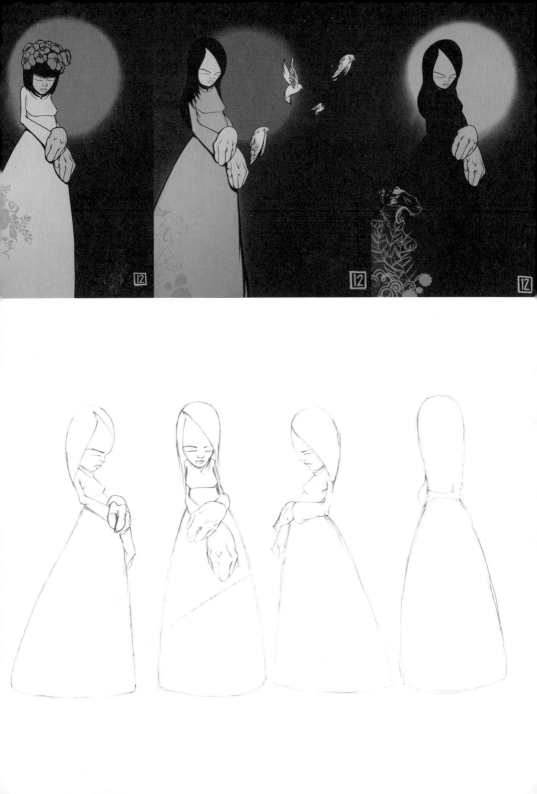

Flores

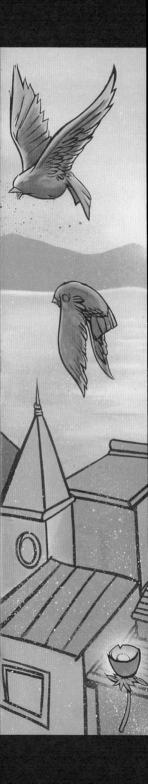

FLORES.04

FLORES

**UPPER
PLAYGROUND**